Teacher's Manual

Creative Writing
For English as
Foreign Language Learners:
A Course Book

Debrah Roundy

Xinghua Liu

Cranmore Publications

A catalogue record for this book is available from the British Library

ISBN: 978-1-907962-84-4

Published by Cranmore Publications

www.cranmorepublications.co.uk

Authors

Native of Idaho, **Prof. Debrah Roundy** graduated from the University of Idaho with a M.Ed. and from NLPU as an NLP Global Trainer. She has been a special education teacher, a developmental specialist, a school consultant and a Neurolinguist. Her research interest is curriculum development and she created much of the curriculum used in her classroom. She has written a book on Neurolinguistic Programs for special needs and elementary school children called "NLP 4 Me." Debrah currently works at Tongji University as a Foreign Language Expert with BYU China Teacher's Program in Shanghai, China.

Dr. Xinghua Liu is a Lecturer in Applied Linguistics at Shanghai Jiao Tong University, China. His research interests include second language writing, corpus linguistics and systemic functional linguistics. Currently, he works as the Chief Editor of TESOL International Journal (www.tesol-international-journal.com).

Preface

Through our teaching experience in various contexts, we found that English as Foreign Language Learners (EFL) normally practice short English writing (about 100 to 250 words) on given general topics. These school-sponsored writing activities are useful in training EFL students to learn fundamental mechanics of English writing and learn vocabulary and grammar. They are also welcomed as EFL students often have to write similar essays for various high-stake language proficiency tests, nationally and internationally. However, by predominantly focusing on this type of essay writing, students are deprived of the opportunity to explore themselves and the outside world through languages. In this fast developing world, we trust it is equally important to distill the sense of creativity and criticality among young learners during the process of learning a foreign language. That said, we hold it necessary to expose our EFL students to various genres and empower them to write them by themselves.

Creative writing is still an elusive term and there has not been a fixed definition. In our teaching practice, we regard any types of writing as creative writing other than those short essays done within time limit and under a writing instruction. Therefore, creative writing in our teaching curriculum may include obituary, poems and CVs.

This book is a result of our work to create a curriculum for the third-year English majors at a Chinese university. Students are exposed to western writing, poetry, writers and authors in the course of the year. Most writing is centered around themselves and their families to help them focus on things that could not be lifted from the internet or other sources. The second term students learn to put together a business packet with business letters, a curriculum vita and a resume. They learned how to cite sources using the MLA style.

We cannot thank more our students in the writing classes who were always keen to gain knowledge, quick to learn, as well as kind and cooperative. We learned while working with them.

This book puts our effective teaching material in a book format. We will continue working on this project and make additions and revisions which will be considered for the next version of the book. Thus, we sincerely welcome all your comments and suggestions.

Prof. Debrah Roundy (droundynlp@gmail.com)

Dr. Xinghua Liu (liuxinghua@sjtu.edu.cn)

Table of Contents

Section 2: In-class Assignments

Introduction

Purpose

This book is written to assist students in writing creatively. Lessons are developed to use the student's own experiences and examples from their own lives and the lives of those around them. As the year progresses students will explore the Neurolinguistic Meta Model to learn to write more concise sentences. They will learn to cite sources and use quotes properly in a document. Students will produce a final project demonstrating creativity and basic writing skills.

Classwork

The lessons are divided into two parts. The first part is to be completed in class. With their peers they will explore quotes and culture, both their own and other cultures. They will show they recognize common errors by finding mistakes in a paragraph or other writing. Additionally they will expand a phrase into a sentence, become famiiar with common English idioms, learn about the Neurolinguistic (NLP) meta model and use it to make their writing more concise and learn to cite common sources quickly to help them with future term papers.

This portion is available for free upload to purchasers of the book by email from either author. Proof of purchase must be emailed in the form of a scanned document. Contacts: droundynlp@gmail.com, 517103484@qq.com, liuxinghua@sjtu.edu.cn.

The second part of the lesson will be homework. Students will have something to write presented each week. Usually it will be based on a personal experience. Each week will include a short reading on the topic of the week, and later on the idiom and meta model pattern students will be working with in class.

Peer editing is an important part of writing in the western culture. Students support and help each other grow. As students edit they will sharpen their skills at finding common mistakes. This will help in their own writing as they become more cognizant of common errors. They will also read other's work and get to know them better. People are so interesting. Soon students will find that they will look eagerly forward to reading and proofing the work of others. It is necessary to bring a colored pen or pencil every week for peer editing.

You as the teacher will decide whether to allow studens to use their electronic gadgets or not.

Discuss it

For the "Discuss It" section students will have a famous quote or a challenge to discuss from their own perspective. They are to use a personal example from their own life or the life of someone they know personally to illustrate or tell about the quote. They are not to substitute a quote of their own liking. They are not to use the quote or any other quote in their essay. You want to see their writing only. I, Debrah, found that the first few weeks I was reading through a vast number of quotes with very few errors but I still did not know if the students could write independently. Therefore I explained that quotes were fine in other classes if allowed by the teacher, but in my class I had a "no quote" policy because I wanted to see their own writing not be grading the writing of the person quoted. The essay is to be timed for five minutes. Then students will count the number of words written. If a student fails to count the words take off points for comprehension. Count words even if they are mistakes for we are looking for the number of words. Students do not stop to use white out on a timed writing, simply cross out the mistakes and move on. Then count the words even though they are crossed out. It is motivating to see how much faster the student can write as the term progresses and students become more fluent in writing in English. Give students one minute before starting to collect their thoughts. On occasion I let them have a five minute discussion about the quote before they started to write to help them generate more ideas as well as just for variety.

When the five minutes are up, write how many words were written in 5 minutes, then, if you choose, students may have 5 minutes more to finish your essay. This should not be a long essay.

The student book has a practice section where students can do a similar practice to the actual in-class assignment. Often the quotes chosen will be similar, one from the Western world and one from the Eastern world. Great minds from the entire world say the same intelligent and perceptive things.

Fix It

This task is to fix the errors in the passage given and assesses basic spelling, punctuation and capitalization skills. Later in the term it may access skills at citing sources, English fluency and similar skills. The skills assessed are often taken from the previous lesson. These skills are chosen from basic skills and from skills that are commonly missed by ESL learners. Students will find it interesting to see how many common mistakes they will soon be catching as their awareness increases. Often there is more than one way to fix the task. There may be a suggested number of mistakes but that is only suggested to give you an idea of how many mistakes you are looking for.

Expand It

Take a simple phrase or sentence and expand it into a sentence by adding to its meaning. It is to be only one sentence long. NO MORE! NO LESS! Often students find the greatest challenge is to write concisely.

The chart below will give you an idea of what you might look for in grading this portion of the class work.

As the teacher look for creativity as well as for errors, here is an example of an "Expand It" graded on a ten point scale.

a girl ran	
0	a woman fast.
	Either student did not do the sentence or did not understand the assignment.
1-2	a litle boy walked
	Sentence is expanded very little and/or there are numerous errors. There is no creativity shown.
3-5	The little boy walked to the store
	The sentence is expanded very little or the expansion lacks creativity. There are numerous errors.
6-8	The little boy who lives next door to me walked happily to the store.
	The sentence shows some good expansion and contains no more than two errors.
8-10	The cute little boy who lives next door to me in the green house walked happily to the store this morning to get her mother some fruit for breakfast.
	The sentence is expanded creatively and has no more than one error.

Challenge It

Into the book, students will be given common metamodel "violations." These come from the study of Neurolinguistic Programs. Although these are really not always violations, they are words that are often not clear to and challenge the reader. This will help students write more concisely so the reading audience can understand more clearly what is written. It is an interesting challenge to lead towards greater clarity. This may be the first time that the Meta Model has been brought to college students in the conteect of a writing class.

Tests/Final

The final test is taken from and laid out as the daily work is.

Students should keep their class papers to help study.

Grading

These as samples of suggested grading rubrics you may choose to use.

Grading Rubric In-Class work

Discuss It	Looking for flow, mechanics and content	50	
Fix It	Mechanics errors including punctuation, grammar and spelling errors	20	
Challenge it	Challenge a meta model pattern writing more concisely (Not in every lesson)	10	
Expand It	creativity, flow and mechanics	10	
Attendance	Attendance is important to learning.	10	
	score	100	

The 5-minute writing with a scale from 1-5.

5-minute Quick Write Essays

	words	development	paragraphs	errors
1	0-40	Little or no Little fluency Very limited vocabulary	No paragraphs May not be on topic	Numerous grammar, mechanical spelling and punctuation errors
2	30-60	Some development Some fluency Limited vocabulary	No paragraphs or supporting topics, in mix matched topics	Grammar, mechanical spelling and punctuation errors
3	50-100	Basic Most sentences fluent Normal vocabulary	1-2 paragraphs On topic Logical organization Average development	Less than 10 grammar, mechanical spelling and punctuation per 100 words
4	80-120	Creates interest fluent Expanded vocabulary	2 or more paragraphs, indented Paragraphs on single topic Indented well developed	Less than 5 grammar, mechanical spelling and punctuation per 100 words
5	100-150	Creatively written No fluency errors Sophisticated vocabulary	2 or more paragraphs, indented, topic sentence and supporting ideas Indented title	No more than one or two errors of grammar, mechanical spelling and punctuation

Section 1

Teacher Help and Directions

Lesson 1: Lesson of Introduction

Purpose

This lesson is to give the teacher an opportunity to assess the students' abilities and needs in writing. It gives the student the opportunity to creatively express himself and let the teacher and class get to know him.

Notes for the Teacher

This Teacher's Edition will have the student assignment and notes for you. Your students will have an in class assignment and also a homework assignment with reading. It is such that a student can do the entire assignment via the internet if you have students out on exchange. The student manual has a reading each week and a student practice assignment that is similar to the in class assignment so students can practice their skills.

Begin the class with an introduction of yourself and the class.Tell students the grading system and what is required of them.

For the Discuss It, tell students:

"Each week for the first term you will have a famous quote to discuss from your own perspective. Use an example from your own life or the life of someone you know personally to illustrate or tell about the quote. Do not use the quote or any other quote in your essay. I want to see your writing only. I will set a timer for 5 minutes. You will write for five minutes starting when I say 'Go.' Then we will count the number of words you wrote. It will be interesting to see how much quicker you can write as the term progresses and you become more fluent in writing in English. I will give you one minute to collect your thoughts before I say 'go.'"

Give students one minute and then start the timer. When it rings you might say, "Write how many words you wrote in 5 minutes, then you may have 5 minutes more to finish your essay. It will be fun to see how much you improve over the term."

For the lesson period go over the MLA style for their first essay. Remind students to bring a colored pen or pencil next week and every week for peer editing.

Learning Activity

An interesting learning activity to prepare students to write their essay is to have the students take out a paper and write down four facts about themselves. Three are true and one is false. They are to be mixed up so no one knows which one it is.

Students then break up into small groups and each person introduces him/herself to the group. Students try to guess which fact is false. Students could do it as an oral presentation, or pass their papers to the next person who marks which one they think is false and then to the next person to guess until the papers have gone all the way around the group. This will give the students a start at organizing ideas that could be used for their essay.

Below is the answer to the first "Fix It".

Fix It

Ann anteater eight andy alligaters apples
sew angy andy Alligator eight ann Anteaters ants?

Answer: Ann Anteater ate Andy Alligator's apples so angry Andy Alligator ate Ann Anteaters ants.

Lesson 2: Character Sketch

Purpose

Students will learn the basics of writing a good character sketch using skills in English writing mechanics, fluency and also character development.

Students will learn to do a good peer edit with a positive affirmation.

Notes for the Teacher

Tell the story of the dolphins.

One day a group of Neurolinguists decided to visit SeaWorld to learn more about learning by studying the way dolphins are trained. It was an enjoyable day and the trainers spent a lot of time with them telling them tips to training a dolphin well. They enjoyed watching the result, too.

Each time the dolphins did the requested trick they would receive a fish. Sometimes there would be several tricks in a row before the dolphin was rewarded. It was obvious the dolphins liked the fish and that the trainers enjoyed rewarding them.

The trainers told the NLP'ers that at first they would watch the dolphin and when the dolphin did something they wanted it to do they would blow a whistle and immediately give the dolphin a fish. The dolphin soon paired the whistle call with a certain behavior such as rolling over, and knew the fish would be coming. Then the fish would stop coming so often and to get another fish the dolphin would have to add another activity such a leap in order to get the fish. Now the dolphin would roll and leap and get a reward. The trainers could get the dolphin to learn an entire pattern of behaviors paired to a whistle blow. The NLP'ers asked many questions and learned that in order to get a fish the dolphin had to perform. No performance, no fish.

Then something magical happened. Now the dolphin knew that something had to be added to the routine and on its own it would add something and then present itself excitedly for a fish. Dolphins are incredible learners and capable of intelligent thinking. Now the dolphin where training their trainers!

It was late in the day and the NLP'ers decided to explore more of SeaWorld as they talked about what they learned. The trainers were teachers, they gave fish. Eventually the students integrated the learning and began explorations on their own.

Closing time was announced and they strolled towards the main gate. They noticed that the gate to the dolphins was open and decided to say a goodbye to their favorite dolphin pals and their trainers. As they entered the area they were surprised to see the trainers just giving the dolphins fish without any tricks. 'What is going on here, I thought the dolphins only got fish for tricks. What is going on?" They demanded to know.

"Oh, these are relation fish," the trainers replied. "The other fish are training fish. We want to keep a good relationship with our dolphins so after performances we give the fish just because we like them."

In class we will peer edit this year. Peer editing is when classmates read the work and look for mistakes. Often when we do our own work we do not see our mistakes. The work has become familiar to us and our eyes automatically put in what is missing or take out what is not needed. Our peers provide a fresh pair of eyes to see both mistakes and the good in our writing. When you peer edit a classmate's work, take the time to write a note of positive affirmation telling what you like about the essay. Sometimes we affectionately call that a fish. You may hear your teacher say, "Write a fish at the bottom of the page." The fish is a positive affirmation statement to keep a good relationship with your peers so you can work together smoothly.

Students will begin to peer edit each other's work. Students take out a colored pen or pencil such as a red, orange, purple or green one. They pass their essay to a peer. Each student then reads the essay and makes a positive comment about it and signs their name(that way if they make a big error on their editing the teacher can help them learn what they need to know by addressing it in class the next week). The student then goes back looking for errors and fixes them. They then pass the papers back.

Depending on how the teacher wants to grade, to encourage good peer editing s/he may give a peer editing bonus point to students who did a good job on their edits and comments. It then encourages them to improve their editing skills.

Class work

Discuss It

Children are our most valuable natural resource.

---Herbert Hoover, 31st president of the USA

Every child born, has innate goodness. – Chinese Proverb

Fix It

daily daphne trainned the dolphines at seeWorld theme park in austin texas

hint World is supposed to be capitalized.

Answer to Fix It

Eleven errors: Daily Daphne trained the dolphins at SeaWorld Theme Park in Austin, Texas.

Lesson 3: Obituaries

Purpose

Students will learn what an obituary is and write one for themselves dreaming big to help them create for themselves a wonderful future.

Notes for the Teacher

Today's lesson is about Neil Armstrong, the first man to walk on the moon. This was such an exciting event in history that the internet is filled with information and short video clips that you can easily access. Show a video clip to the students and talk about what it meant to have a person do something that had never been done before. Talk about the effect of a life on others. It a well-known person has recently died in the country you are teaching in or your home land, you could add that to the lecture to make it more interesting and pertinent to the students. Then have your students start the class work.

Learning Activity

Have each student write down three things they would like to do during their stay here on earth. Challenge them to dream and dream big. After they have written three things down, invite them to share with a friend. Studies have shown that people who write down their dreams and share them with others are more likely to realize those dreams.

Notes

Customs and laws of how to respect the dead and to dispose of their remains vary throughout the world. Tell students about customs from the place you come from. You might want to address what is done to the body to preserve it or is it preserved, how and for how long does the family mourn, and what is the correct way to show sympathy and respect. Address how the death is announced and what kinds of clothes are customary to wear when a person is in mourning. Tell the students if they are in a foreign land and someone they know dies, to ask a person in that place whom they respect for advice so they will make the appropriate social actions to properly respect the person and the culture.

Class Work

Today's lesson is about Neil Armstrong, the first man to walk on the moon. If you are not able to come to class, look up information about Mr. Armstrong on the internet before you start your assignment.

Discuss It

This is one small step for man, one giant leap for mankind. ---Neil Armstrong

Fix It

neil armstrng the american astronaut who said   one giant leap for mankind when he became the first man to walk on the moon died saturday august 25 2012

Answer to Fix it

Neil Armstrong, the American astronaut who said, "One giant leap for mankind" when he became the first man to walk on the moon, died Saturday, August 25, 2012.

Lesson 4: Giving Directions

Purpose

Students will share their culture by writing about a holiday they have had.

Notes for the Teacher

Talkabout a recent holiday you had or a holiday that is important to your culture. Share pictures of your holiday. If you are from a different culture make it an interesting culture share. Then tell the students you would like to learn more about their cultural celebrations. Every culture and even every family has different traditions. This is a good time to share cultures and help students understand that every culture is interesting.

Instruct the students on the use of first person. Tell them that this is to be from their own experience so they will use the words *I, me and my*. Ask them to explain what makes their story unique. Do they do things differently than others in other cultures? Did they do something unique to their own experience? Did something unusual happen? Make their story a fun and interesting read.

Learning Activity

Have the students write down four things that people could see or visit if they went to their home town. Divide into groups and have each group pass the papers around to one another and write down their guess of what city each student comes from. If many of the students all come from the same place or if they know each other well, instead challenge them to write four things about a city they have visited.

Fix It

My professor seen a lot ov sites during the mid autumn festival held in china when the harvest moon are hear

Answer to Fix It

10-11 errors: My professor saw a lot of sights (sites) during the Mid-Autumn Festival held in China when the harvest moon is here.

Lesson 5: Writing Directions to Do a Thing

Purpose

Students will share their abilities and/or culture by writing clear directions about something they do well.

Notes for the Teacher

Start the class by talking about talents. Have each student write a talent of theirs that they think no one knows on a piece of paper. Pass them in. Read the papers and have the students try to guess which student it is. Then start the class work.

Learning Activity

After the class work, introduce the subject of writing directions.Choose an activity that is familar to English Culture but not to the culture you teach in. Making a peanut butter sandwich is a great American one. Putting together a taco would be fun for a Mexican teacher. After you finish the activity you could have samples for all of the students to try if that is allowed in the place you are at. Do check on local laws before you bring food to a classroom. Here are directions.

Have one student watch you make a peanut butter sandwich or do someother simple task indicative of your culture. Do it so that the other students do not see or do it silently so you have given the student no words. Next blindfold the student who will give the directions so he cannot see what you are doing.Have the student give directions to make the sandwich while blind folded. Folllow the directions completely as the student gives them. If something is left out, leave it out also. For instance if the students says take the bread, take the whole loaf, unwrapped. Have fun with the demonstration. Last, lead the discussion into what are good directions.

Answer to Fix It

This is one way to fix the assignment.

Directions from the Post Office to the Rupert Square

1. Exit the post office. You are on F Street.
2. Turn to your left (south).
3. Go two blocks on F Street.
4. You are now at the Rupert Square.
5. If you need help, just call me at 208-123-4567

Post office is capitalized in the title but not in the directions because there it is a common noun.

The student could use a colon (:) before the phone number.

Lesson 6: Descriptive Essay

Purpose

Students will show they understand basic vocabulary for ordering events in the Fix It section. Students will show understanding of a descriptive essay and how to put a title on an essay in MLP format.

Notes for the Teacher

To open the lesson talk to the students about your hometown and what you like about it. Explain how a good essay paints a word picture with descriptive language.

If you have obtained the power point there is something called a FYI. This stands for "For Your Information," and is a note with information on it that is not included on the test and is not needed to complete the assignment but gives the reader a broader understanding. The FYI is on the difference between different urban and city areas of the United States.

FYI: (For your information). A village is generally smaller than a town which is smaller than a city. A city is incorporated and legally defined as a government entity with power given to the city by the people and providing services to the people. Power may include the power to create roads. Services may be building good roads for the people of the community.

Learning Activity

Students write down three sentences telling about their home town. Divide the students in groups paired with others they do not know well. Have each group try to guess where the hometown is of each member in the group. If all are from the same home town, have them write about a place they have visited.

You might want to let them have three guesses. If they get it in three guesses they win. If it takes more than three then the Cat wins. The cat means that no one wins.

Class work

Today you get to share about your home town or a town or city you have visited.

Answer to Fix It

How to Receive a Gift

First, accept the gift.

Second, say thank you.

Third, open the gift.

Last say thank you again.

Other options.

Students could also use firstly, secondly and thirdly.

Students could instead use quotation marks like this: say, "Thank you."

Lesson 7: The Friendly Letter

Purpose

The students will demonstate their knowledge of how to write a title by fixing several titles. Students will write a friendly letter to the person of their choice.

Notes for the Teacher

To introduce the lesson talk with the students about the importance of a handwritten letter. Emails have just about taken over the world of writing but sometimes there is nothing that compares with the thoughtfulness of a handwritten letter. Letters that are handwritten are often kept as treasures and become family keepsakes handed down from generation to generation as a treasure of the family.

Encourage the students to choose an ordinary person, one they love or respect, and write a letter to that person. After they are graded, encourage the student to give a copy to the person they wrote to. Sometimes it can be fun to write a letter to someone who has passed on just to keep as a tender memory.

Learning Activity

Present each student with a picture. The pictures could be from old calendars or postcards. Each student then writes three short, descriptive sentences about the picture that s/he has. Collect the pictures and display them on a table. Collect the sentences and mix them up. Students then put the sentences they received with the picture they believe it matches. After all pictures are matched the students read the sentence and the class listens to see if they agree.

Answer to Fix It

A History of the Oriental Tradesman

The Life of Joshua D. Roundy

It's a Long Road to Beijing

There are 15 errors

Lesson 8: Formal Emails

Purpose

Students will show they can understand the basic format of a friendly letter by fixing one with numerous errors. Students will learn the basics of a formal email. Students will learn to do a good peer edit with a positive affirmation.

Notes for the Teacher

Introduce the lesson by talking about technology. You might ask the students how many own smart phones, a computer, an Ipad or similar device. Ask them how different their lives would be without the use of technology.

Technology was not always present in the lives of people and people developed skills to make a society run smoothly. One of those skills was letter writing. Nowdays almost every student can text and email. Those applications are rarily used formally by the student but increasingly are being used by the business world and the social world. There is a need for a formal email. Ask the students when a formal email might be used and elicit responses such as a thank you note, a note to your boss or to another company and when applying or a job, which increasingly is being done on line. A formal email is an important skill for students to aquire for future success.

Learning Activities

Students do a lot of texting. In small groups pass out a copy of the testing symbols worksheet. Let the groups decode them to read the messages. Students will be working with western style poetry next week. It is good for them to become familiar with rhyming words. Put up a word on the board and have the students come up with as many words as possible that rhyme with that word. This will not only be a good exercise for the students, but will tell you assess their knowledge of rhyming words. Here are some good choices:

cat	rut	pet	sit	rot	ran	can
Sam	seat	soil	ape	site	roam	

Pass the handout below to your students and let then figure out what each message is as a small group.

u nd 2 sqsh ur wrds 2 cnsrvspce

SUP WAN2 go out 2nite

IDK WAN2 GO 2 TOWN

LOL no time WBU

IDC WBU

2moro bbq

BBQ 2MORO then, BCNU BFF

Answers to the activity

| u nd 2 sqsh ur wrds 2 cnsrvspce |
| You need to squash your words to conserve space. |

| SUP WAN2 go out 2nite |
| What's up? Do you want to go out tonight? |

| IDK WAN2 GO 2 TOWN |
| I don't know. Want to go to town? |

| LOL no time WBU |
| Laugh, no time, What about you? |

| IDC WBU |
| I don't care. What about you? |

| 2moro bbq |
| Tomorrow let's go to a barbecue? |

| BBQ 2MORO then, BCNU BFF |
| Barbecue tomorrow then. I'll be seeing you. Best Friends forever. |

Text messages are limited to 160 characters. This includes letters, numbers and spaces. You need to conserve space. Using abbreviation and texting shortcuts will help you do just that.

RUOK	are you ok?	CUL8R	see you later	IMO	in my opinion
b	be	THNQ	thank you	SFSG	so far so good
BRB	be right back	TY	thank you	WTG	way to go
BCNU	be seeing you	YW	you are welcome	BTW	by the way
BFN	bye for now	2	to too	NP	no problem
<J>	joking	2day	today	GG	good game
FYI	for your information	2MORO	tomorrow	NM	never mind (forget it)
BBQ	barbeque	2nite	tonight	JK	just kidding
BFF	best friends forever	WAN2	want 2	XOXO	hugs and kisses
BF	boy friend	SUP	what's up	CYA	see you (goodbye)
GF	girl friend	IDC	I don't care	PLZ	please
DW	dear wife	uok	are you ok?	GJ	good job
DH	dear husband	IDK	I don't know	ASL	age, sex, location
DS	dear son	LOL	laughing out loud	BSLY	but I still love you
DD	dear daughter	:D	laugh	ADDY	address
DB	dear brother	KK	okay	B4N	bye for now
MIL	mother in law	WBU	what about you	RUOK	are you ok?

Answers to fix It

402 East 16 Street
Rupert, Id. 83350
October 16, 2013

Dear Grandma,
Indent~~and~~Last week I went to the fabric market,~~and~~Century Park and Pizza Hut.~~and~~Then I visited with my friend Suzi from Idaho. ~~in a word~~It was a wonderful and exciting experience

Yours,
Professor Roundy

There are a lot of mistakes and there is more than one way to fix it. This version has 28 errors. Many students use "In a word" followed by many words. In a word means just that, one word. Be careful not to get caught in that trap.

Lesson 9: Western Culture: Halloween

Purpose

Students will be introduced to a popular minor western holiday, Halloween. This will lead to writing a simple poem.

Notes for the Teacher

Introduce the western holiday of Halloween. Halloween is always October 31 and if it is near your lesson time you might move this lesson up or back to accommodate the holiday. Give the students a brief history of Halloween. Use the information below if it is an unfamiliar holiday to your culture.

A BRIEF HISTORY OF HALLOWEEN

By Debrah Roundy
Pictures from Microsoft Clip Art

Halloween is a minor holiday celebrated on the night of October 31. Students do not get out of school and businesses continue their usual work for the day on a minor holiday. Traditional activities include trick-or-treating, bonfires, parties, dressing in costumes, visiting "haunted houses" and carving jack-o-lanterns.

Halloween has its origins in the ancient Celtic festival known as Samhain (pronounced "sah-win"), a harvest celebration. The ancient Gaels believed that on October 31, the boundaries between the worlds of the living and the dead overlapped and the deceased would come back to life and cause havoc such as sickness or damaged crops. Therefore the festival would frequently involve bonfires to scare them away. It is believed that the fires attracted insects to the area which then attracted bats to eat the insects. These are additional attributes of the history of Halloween.

Trick-or-treating, is a popular activity for children on or around Halloween. Children go from door to door in costumes, asking for treats. They knock on the door and say out, "Trick or treat?" The "trick" part of "trick or treat" is a threat to play a trick on the homeowner or his property if no treat is given. Trick-or-treating is one of the main traditions of Halloween. It has become socially expected that if one lives in a neighborhood with children one should purchase treats such as small candy, in preparation for trick-or-treaters. Your author Debrah thinks that American children get altogether too much candy so hands out pencils or other small trinkets instead.

A jack-o'-lantern (sometimes also spelled Jack O'Lantern) is typically a carved pumpkin however apples, gourds and even turnips have been used. Typically the top is cut off, and the inside flesh then scooped out. An image, usually a face, is carved onto the outside surface, and the lid replaced. During the night, a candle is placed inside to illuminate the face with a spooky, eerie glow. The term is not particularly common outside North America, although the practice of carving lanterns for Halloween is.

An Irish folk tale says that Jack, a lazy but clever farmer, was getting chased by some villagers from whom he had stolen something, when he met the Devil, who claimed it was time for Jack to die. However, the thief stalled his death by tempting the Devil with a chance to bedevil the church-going villagers chasing him. Jack told the Devil who could turn into any shape he wanted to turn into a coin with which he would pay for the stolen goods. Later, when the coin/Devil disappeared, the Christian villagers would fight over who had stolen it. The Devil agreed to this plan. He turned himself into a silver coin and jumped into Jack's wallet, only to find himself next to a cross Jack had also picked up in the village and craftily planted there. Jack had closed the wallet tight, and the cross stripped the Devil of his powers for the devil cannot cross a cross. Ireland, being a Christian nation believed that the cross of Jesus has tremendous power as it represented the goodness of Jesus who promised to die on the cross innocently to pay for the sins of all mankind. The cross came to represent the ultimate goodness. The Devil was trapped. Jack only lets the Devil go when he agrees never to take Jack's soul. After a while Jack died, as all living things do. Of course, his life had been too sinful for Jack to go to heaven, however, the Devil had promised not to take his soul, and so he was barred from Hell as well. Jack now had nowhere to go. He asked how he would see where to go, as he had no light, and the Devil mockingly tossed him an ember that would never burn out from the flames of hell. Jack carved out one of his turnips (which were his favorite food), put the ember inside it, and began endlessly wandering the Earth for a resting place. He became known as "Jack of the Lantern", or Jack-o'-Lantern.

Halloween costumes are uniquely different from costumes for other celebrations. They are often designed to imitate supernatural or scary beings. Costumes are traditionally those of monsters such as vampires, ghosts, skeletons, witches, and devils. There are also costumes of pop culture figures like presidents, or film, television, and cartoon characters.

What would dress up like if you had a choice?

Learning Activity

At the end of this lesson are several games to give your students more information about Halloween. This will build their vocabulary and stretch their skills. The first is to see how many words can be made from Halloween. Here are the directions for the game.

HOW MANY WORDS CAN YOU MAKE FROM THE WORD "HALLOWEEN"?

This activity is used to increase vocabulary. Take a word that is a big word with many letters. Try to find smaller words made of the same letters as the big word. See how many small words you can find. At the end of the time the person with the most words is the winner. The activity leader has everyone stand up. Then she calls out numbers starting with one. When s/he gets to your number you sit down. The last person standing is the winner. It is ok to check with your dictionary to make sure the word you chose was a real word. Here are some simple examples:

cats
cats, cat, sat, at, a, as   6 words
lamb
lamb, am, ma, a, lab, am   6 words

How to Play Bingo

This is a good activity to work on vocabulary. Students listen to the words and how they are pronounced. The teacher should explain each word as it comes up. S/he can do them in any order. It is nice to have a bag of small candies, pencils or other trinkets to give to the winners.

Each card has a word bank with many vocabulary words. There is also a grid with 25 spaces. Choose 25 of those words and put them in the spaces.

When it is time to start, students listen for the words as the teacher calls them out and explains what the word means. When a word the student has chosen is on the activity card, the student crosses it out. There are 13 winners. The first to get all five in one row across. ↔ The first to get all 5 in one row up and down, and the first to get all five from corner to corner both top to bottom and bottom to top \ / . Also winners are the first student to get a letter from LUCKY T, a +, and a frame. The student who is the first raises his/her hand and says "Bingo!"

The final winner is the first to get the whole activity card crossed out. That is called black out. The person with the blackout raises her/his hand and says "Black out." Usually the activity is over but sometimes one of the other ways is not done and the game continues if the teacher desires.

Unless there are a small number of students, each student can only win once at Bingo but they are still in the game for Black Out.

Answers to Fix It

Five little pumpkins

5 little pumpkins sitting on a gate

the 1ˢᵗ won said oh my its getting lat

the second one said, "there are witches in the air"

the 3ʳᵈ won said but we don't care

the 4ᵗʰ one said lets run and runand run

the 5ᵗʰ one said im ready for some fun

oh-hh went the wind and out went the lites

and the 5 little pumpkins roled out of site

Five Little Pumpkins
Five little pumpkins sitting on a gate,
The first one said, "Oh, my, it's getting late."
The second one said, "There are witches in the air."
The third one said, "But we don't care."
The fourth one said, "Let's run and run and run."
The fifth one said, "I'm ready for some fun!"
Oh, hh went the wind and out went the light,
And the five little pumpkins rolled out of sight.

HALLOWEEN BINGO

Fill out the Bingo cards with whatever 25 words you randomly choose and as the leader calls out the words, you are to X out the words you have on their card. You are trying to get five in a row, up and down, sideways, diagonally, a through the middle, a frame or the letters to LUCKY T. We will play 13 games like that, the first to get it each way. Then the last game is blackout. You can only win at BINGO once but you are still in the game for BLACKOUT. Black Out happens when someone gets all of the words that have been called.   Choose from these words:

bat	bewitch	bizarre	black cat	boo!
broomstick	cauldron	costume	creepy	devil
frighten	ghost	goblin	goodies	gotcha!
ghouls	Halloween	Haunt	mask	horror movies
howl	jack-o-lantern	macabre	magic	haunted house
monster	morbid	mummy	owl	pumpkin
skeleton	skull	spell	spider	spirit
spook alley	trick-or-treat	vampire	warlock	werewolf
witch	witches' brew	apples	candy	scream

⟷ ⇕ \ / X + L U C K Y T ☐ ■

HOW MANY WORDS CAN YOU MAKE FROM THE WORD "HALLOWEEN"?

#		#	
1		17	
2		18	
3		19	
4		20	
5		21	
6		22	
7		23	
8		24	
9		25	
10		26	
11		27	
12		28	
13		29	
14		30	
15		31	
16		32	

HALLOWEEN VOCABULARY

apples- round fruit that ripens in the falls and is often eaten around Halloween time

bat – small flying animal that eats insects and fruit, can live in caves

bewitch – to cast a spell, to enchant, to influence by using witchcraft

bizarre – strange, odd, very unusual

black cat – thought to be a companion to a witch, to the superstitious is said to be bad luck

boo! – an exclamation used to frighten or startle

broomstick – the long thin handle of a broom on which a witch and cat ride

Candy- sweet treats usually made with a lot of sugar

cauldron – a large kettle, a pot witches could use to make a witch brews of an evil potion (drink)

costume – clothing worn as a disguise

creepy – producing a nervous, eerie, frightened feeling as to bring chills up one's spine

devil – the supreme spirit of evil, the ruler of hell

frighten – to make afraid

ghost – the spirit of a dead person

ghoul – a legendary evil being that robs graves

goblin – an ugly spirit that is usually mischievous and sometimes evil

goodies - sweets, candy

gotcha! – an unexpected embarrassment or funny moment when someone takes you by surprise.

Halloween – October 31, a celebration of All Saints Eve

haunt – when a ghost visits a place

haunted house – an old house decorated to frighten visitors on Halloween

horror movies – scary movies

howl – the long mournful cry of dogs and wolves

jack-o-lantern – a lantern made of a pumpkin cut to look like a human face

macabre – having to do with death

magic – the use of charms or spells to gain power over natural forces

mask – a disguise used to cover or partially cover the face

monster – a being of unnatural or extreme ugliness, wickedness or cruelty

morbid – abnormally gloomy or unwholesome feelings

mummy – a body treated for burial in the manner of the ancient Egyptians

owl – a nocturnal (awake at nighttime) bird with a large head that can turn 270 degrees

pumpkin – a large, round, orange fruit of the gourd family

skeleton – the bony framework of the body

skull – the bones of the head, it protects the brain

spell – spoken words thought to have magic power

spider – an arachnid with a body divided into two and four pairs of legs

spirit – a supernatural being or essence

spook alley – rooms decorated to frighten visitors

trick-or-treat – children's Halloween practice of asking for treats when going from door to door under threat of playing tricks on those who refuse

vampire – dead person who comes from the grave at night to suck the blood of sleeping living beings

warlock – a man practicing black witchcraft often with the aid of the devil

werewolf – a person who turns into a wolf or takes on a wolf's form

<u>witch</u> – a woman practicing black witchcraft often with the aid of the devil
<u>witches' brew</u>– a strong, powerful drink made by a witch

WORDS YOU CAN MAKE FROM "HALLOWEEN"

a	heal	lea	own
ale	heel	leal	wale
all	hell	lean	wall
allow	hello	lee	we
alone	hen	loan	wean
an	ho	lone	well
aw	hoe	low	whale
awl	hole	new	wheel
eel	hon	no	when
ell	hone	now	who
eon	how	oh	whoa
ha	howl	ole	whole
hale	la	on	woe
hall	lane	one	won
hallow	law	owe	
haw	lawn	owl	

Lesson 10: Poetry

Purpose

Students asked what the parts of a fruit were. This lesson grew out of that question.

Notes for the Teacher

To introduce the lesson talk about parts of an orange using English words to build vocabulary.

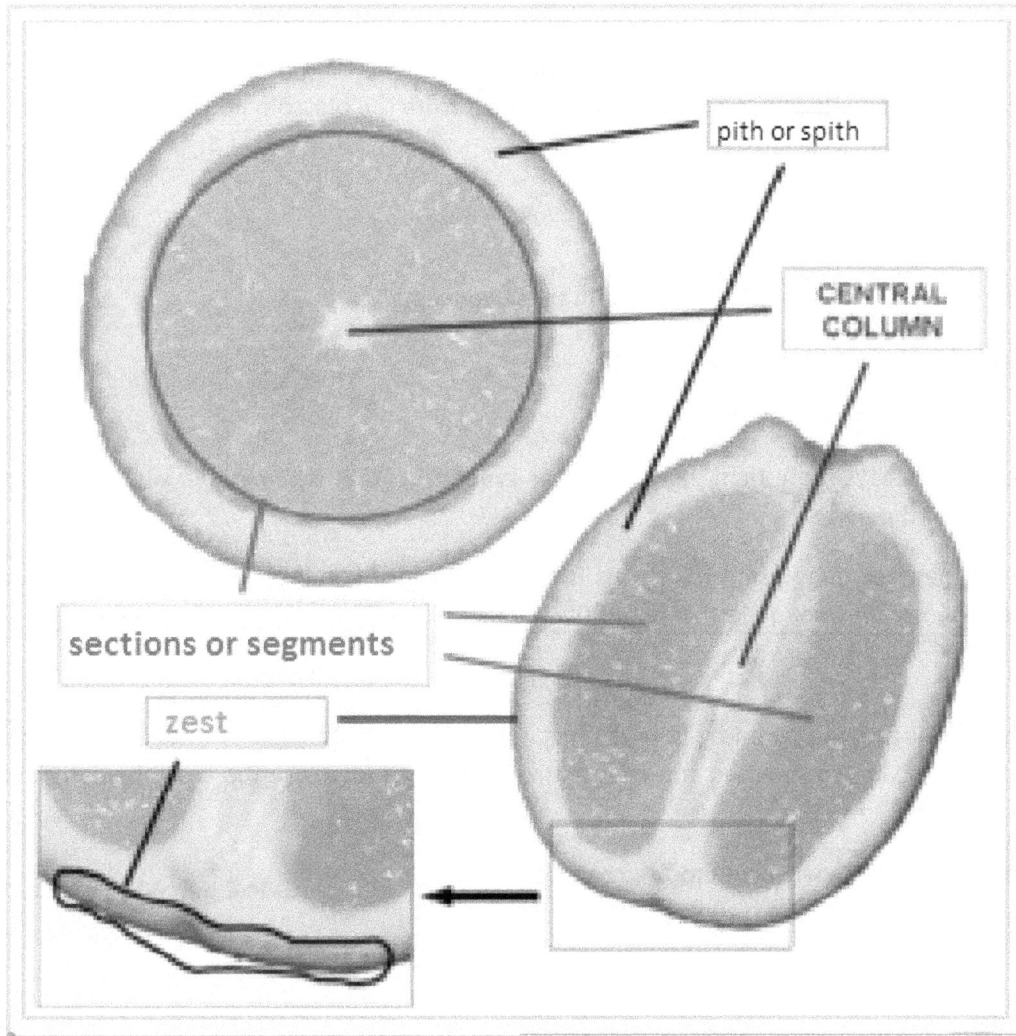

Juice is the liquid in the sections. Pulp is what is left after the juice is extracted or taken out.

After students have written their Discuss it quick write, and peer edited them if you choose. Introduce the Meta model challenge. Students will encounter a Meta model challenge for the first time in this week's lesson. Start by putting this sentence on the board:

You **must** eat an orange every day to be healthy.

Point out the model operator of necessity, must. Ask students to come up with challenges for this sentence. Some ideas include:

If I don't eat an orange every day can I still be healthy?
Must I eat an orange, could I eat an apple instead?
Why must I eat an orange, I am allergic to them.
I do not like oranges, must I eat an orange.
Could I drink a glass of orange juice instead?

Here are sample answers for the challenge, *It is necessary to peel your orange from the stem.*

Why is it necessary to peel the orange from the stem?
What would happen if I did not peel the orange from the stem?
I want to make an orange flower and for that I must peel it from the blossom end.
Will the flavor change if I peel it from the other end?

Learning Activity

Introduce the students to the poetry section with these concepts.

- Generally western poetry has a rhythm

- Western poetry generally rhymes

- Poetry often says more than the words, it is synergistic, that is the whole is greater than the sum of the parts

- Poetry may not obey usual rules; this is called taking poetic license. This is often used when a word does not quite rhyme but fits the meaning of the poem.

Continue by introducing the poem by Robert Frost, "The Road not Taken." Take to the students about a choice you had and the road you choose. If you need an idea, use the essay below. Have the students:

- Write about a time when you took a road less taken.

- What was your road?

- Are you glad you did?

- What happened because you took that road?

- Share your writing with a friend. Comment on the writing that is shared with you.

Answers to Fix It

Pith contains the fiber we need to keep our bodies healthy. It provides the antioxidants our bodies need to fight diseases like cancer. 11 errors (mistakes).

The Road Not Taken

- Robert Frost

Two roads diverged in a yellow wood,
And sorry I could not travel both
And be one traveler, long I stood
And looked down one as far as I could
To where it bent in the undergrowth;

Then took the other, as just as fair,
And having perhaps the better claim
Because it was grassy and wanted wear,
Though as for that the passing there
Had worn them really about the same,

And both that morning equally lay
In leaves no step had trodden black.
Oh, I marked the first for another day!
Yet knowing how way leads on to way
I doubted if I should ever come back.

I shall be telling this with a sigh
Somewhere ages and ages hence:
Two roads diverged in a wood, and I,
I took the one less traveled by,
And that has made all the difference.

Sample Essay

My Road Taken --- By Debrah Roundy

Like Robert Frost I was at a path that diverged. I had retired. I could do what most people do, stay home, play cards, chat with the neighbors and lead an ordinary life. Or, I could take the road less taken and come to China on a quest to make the world a better place by sharing English skills.

I would like to think that I may have that choice again, but I may not. I am getting older and I do not know how long my life will be.

Making that choice there is one thing I am sure of, that it will make a difference. My grandchildren will find the world is a smaller and more friendly place for the time I spent teaching in China.

Lesson 11: Writing a Pro/Con Essay

Purpose

Students will show they understand the use of articles in the Fix It this week. They will write an essay looking at both sides of an argument.

Notes for the Teacher

Introduce the classwork by talking about your family either your spouse and children or the family you grew up in. Tell a story about something that happened to your family or something you did together. Talk about helping your children with their work or being helped by your own parents and how important that is to future success. Then begin the classwork.

The discussion today is on a pattern called Logical Level Alignment. It was developed by Neurolinguists and comes from the work of Gregory Bateson. Bateson noticed that there are natural hierarchies of classification. Each level organizes the information on the level below. As we move up the levels each level embodies the previous level while adding a new dimension. Students will use this LLA format for their essay. Below are the levels of the LLA. Notice that we start at the bottom with the environment and move up the levels to the purpose which is the pinnacle or peak of the issue. As students work through this LLA they will find that it helps them organize ideas and arguments effectively. They can use these to very effectively write their essays and will find that the essay will flow easily from the form.

```
                    ▲
                    │
                   ╱│╲
                  ╱ │ ╲
                 ╱Purpose╲
                ╱───┆────╲
               ╱    ┆     ╲
              ╱  Identity  ╲
             ╱─────┆───────╲
            ╱      ┆        ╲
           ╱ Beliefs & Values╲
          ╱───────┆──────────╲
         ╱        ┆           ╲
        ╱    Capabilities      ╲
       ╱─────────┆─────────────╲
      ╱          ┆              ╲
     ╱       Behavior            ╲
    ╱──────────┆──────────────────╲
   ╱           ┆                   ╲
  ╱        Environment              ╲
 ╱────────────┆─────────────────────╲
```

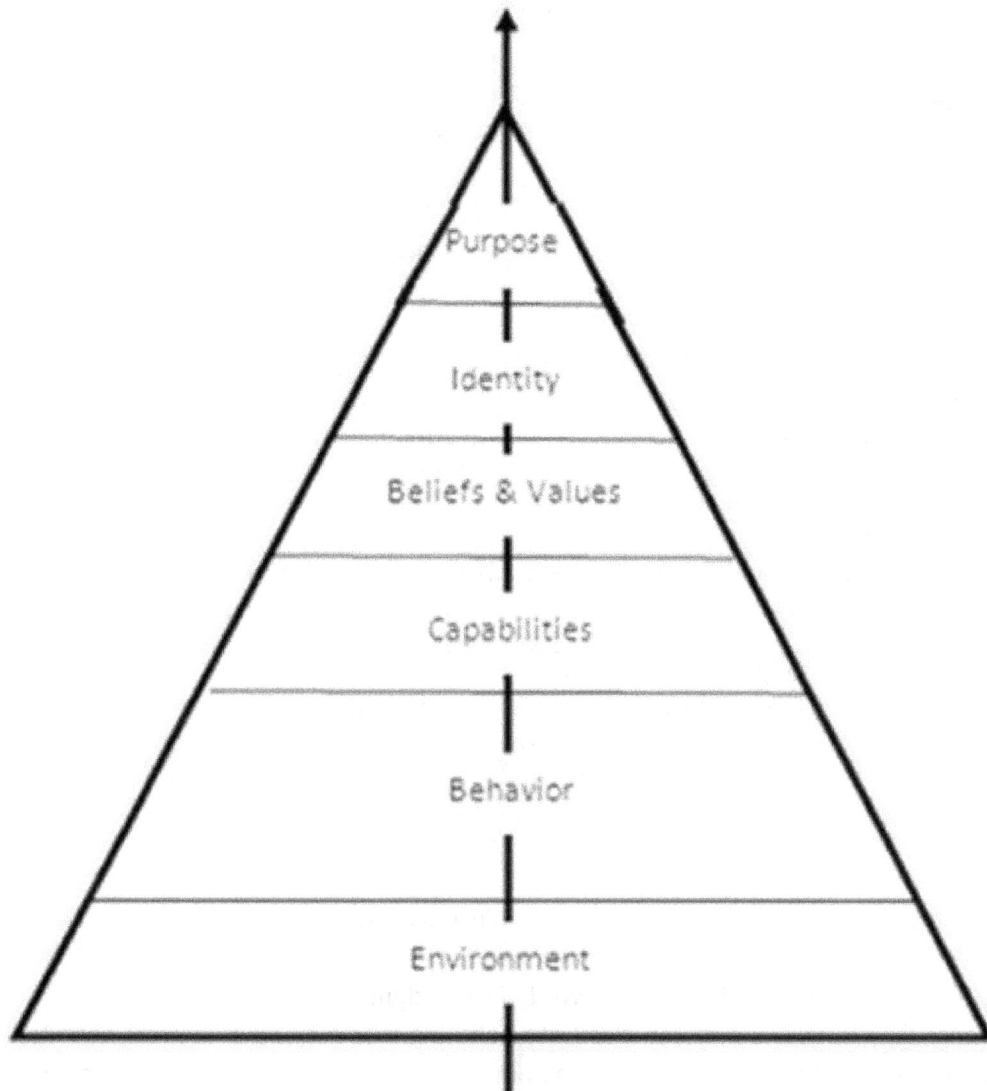

Here is an explanation of those levels

	answers
	answers
Environment	Answers the questions when and where. Often environment includes the senses. What do you see, hear, feel, taste and smell at the place here you are
Behavior	Answers *What?* The actions and reactions to the environment
Capability	Answers *How? What* strategies are used?
Beliefs and values	Answers *why* we do the things we do?
	the values and meanings a person or organization puts on things in life
Identity	Answers **Who** am I?
Purpose	Answers the questions "For Whom" or "For what?" Purpose reaches beyond our body and into the greater field of time and space.

Work through the chart with a pro/con issue such as coming to English writing class vs. sleeping in. Here are some ideas to help you if needed.

Coming to English Writing Class vs. Sleeping In		
	pro	Con
Environment	classroom on time	the bed, so soft and warm
Behavior	sitting in class greeting friends, taking out materials, listening and writing	sleeping
Capability	I can write and read English	I can get adequate sleep for my body
Beliefs and values	It is important to be to class and to get good grades	It is important to get adequate sleep for good health
	Good grades are valuable to my future	staying healthy is valuable to my heath
Identity	I am a person who gets good grades because I attend my classes.	I am a person who stays healthy because I get adequate sleep.
Purpose	I want to get a good job to support my family in the future.	I want to be healthy so I can work hard at my job in the future so I can support my family.

Learning Activity

Fake It. This is a learning activity that is a lot of fun and increases vocabulary also. The teacher has four students come up. Each is given a paper with one word on it. Three papers only have the word but the fourth has the definition of the word. The students who do not have a definition make up one that they think will trick the class into believing that they have the real definition. They might want to act as if they are reading it and act confident. The student with the definition just reads the real definition but may also try to "fake the class out" into thinking they do not have it by acting as if they are making it up as they go along. The class then tries to guess who has the real definition.

Handouts and Activity Sheets

Words for Fake It. These words are all related to families.

nuclear	nuclear
nuclear	nuclear the family unit of just two parents and their own children
extended	extended a family unit made of parents, children and other relatives such as grandparents
extended	extended
first cousin "once removed"	first cousin "once removed"
first cousin "once removed"	first cousin "once removed" your grandparent's first cousin
removed	removed
removed	removed a generational term showing how many generations apart you are from a common ancestor

Answers to Fix It

in english their are too kinds of articles definate (the)
and indefinate (a and an)   the is used for a specific
item and a or an is used to refer to a item
tri these sample
the family is going on a outing
an family is going on the outing

Circle the sentence that tells a specific family.

Depending on how you choose to fix it, and there is more than one way, there will be between 16 and 24 errors. The writing is set up properly. All errors are mechanical errors.

In English there are two kinds of articles, definite (the) and indefinite (a and an). "The" is used for a specific item and "a" or "an" is used to refer to an item.

Try these samples:

The family is going on an outing.
A family is going on the outing.
Point out to students that "the" refers to something definite therefore it is the definite article. "A" and "an" refer to something that is not definite so they are indefinite articles. This may help them remember.

Lesson 12: Copyrights

Purpose

The students will learn about copyright laws and the importance of respecting the author or artist by giving credit where it should be given for intellectual property. Students will learn the basic Haiku poetry form and learn to recognize the Crystal Ball Meta Model pattern.

Notes for the Teacher

Start the class by telling a story of someone in the music industry who has worked hard to produce a song. Similarly a story could be told of a software developer as these artists are both targeted often. The money he makes from his song will help feed his family. Soon after it is published many people pirate (use his song for money gaining purposes, theft) his song illegally to down load and enjoy. He would like to write music full time and devote his life to it, but because of pirated copies he does not make enough money to support himself and his family. Then discuss the importance of copyright laws.

Illegally downloading a song may not feel like a crime, after all, you want it. But it is a serious crime and the accumulative impact of millions of songs downloaded illegally is devastating. Not only does it hurt the musicians who write and produce the songs, but also all of the other people in the music industry who help to bring the songs to the fans. The Institute for Policy Innovation did a study that showed that the annual harm to the U.S. economy amounts to twelve and a half billion dollars as well as 70,000 lost jobs and $2 billion dollars in lost wages to American workers. Other countries face similar loses.

Copyright Laws. A copyright is literally that, the right to make copies. In the United States the concept of protecting artists, authors and/or inventors' exclusive right to benefit from their work comes directly from Article I, Section 8 of the United States Constitution. It is a law.

"The Congress shall have Power ... To promote the Progress of Science and useful Arts, by securing for limited Times to Authors and Inventors the exclusive Right to their respective Writings and Discoveries"

Other countries also have similar laws. A good source for International Copyright **laws is**MegaLaw.com. It offers links to copyright laws from all over the world.

As a teacher you may wonder how copyright laws affect you directly. The United States has Fair Use laws that allow a teacher and students to use portions of copyrighted work for educational purposes. The teacher should be careful to use only portions and copyrighted materials should not be used in publishing without the author's permission. Sites such at Purdue OWL will allow you to make copies of their material for educational purposes by simply writing and asking their permission. Other sites such as templetons.com allow teachers to make a certain number of copies without permission. Teachers are examples to their students and should take the time to cite their sources and ask permission for the materials they use when it is required.

Learning Activity

Hot Seat: a game for developing descriptive skills

-a whiteboard
- two chairs in front of the whiteboard
-place the chairs in front of the whiteboard, with the backs facing the board.

The Activity

This is an easy game to play and once you get into it, students simply won't want to stop! Divide the class into two teams, with a few feet of space dividing the teams in the middle.

Pick a student from each team to sit in the chairs, otherwise known as "the hot seats". They will not be able to see the board, so stress the fact that they are not allowed to turn around and look at it.

To start the game, have a practice run. Write a simple word on the board like "apple", and then explain to the class that they need to elicit this word from their teammate in the hot seat. They can say anything they want, except the word on the board. No spelling, No acting. They must get them to say the word by explaining it to them in as much detail as possible.

For apple, they might say something like "it's one word, it's a red fruit, and it grows on trees," etc.

Once they get how it works, start the game! I usually let each pair of students in the hot seats have a few turns before changing the students up. It usually takes a couple words for them to really get into it. For beginner classes, simple words are good. For advanced classes, add phrases and then you can get as complicated as you want! It's surprising how good they will become at explaining words or concepts to their teams.

Once one of the people in the hot seat says the correct word or phrase, give that team a point and immediately write a new word on the board so you don't lose momentum.

You may add a few joke sentences in the mix with more advanced groups, such as "My boyfriend is a gorilla" or "My teacher is the smartest in the world" to keep the mood fun and the class laughing. A good reward for the winning team is to let them leave the classroom first.

Answers to Fix It

of the goods made for apple, most are made in china? once
apple s brand is added to it and it is exported to the united
states it's value doubles   he sayed   ---by ben blanchard

18 errors: "**O**f the goods made for Apple, most are made in China. Once Apple's brand is added to it and it is exported to the United States its value doubles," he said. ---By Ben Blanchard

Lesson 13: Thanksgiving and *A Christmas Carol*

Purpose

Students will learn about the United States and Canadian holiday of Thanksgiving. Students will start to read *"A Christmas Carol,"* by Charles Dickens. In Canada the holiday is held in October. In the United States it is the fourth Thursday in November.

Notes for the Teacher

As each student has written a Haiku poem for homework, have them share their poem with several other students. Each student writes a positive affirmation then all Haikus are returned to the students to read their affirmations before being handed in.

After the students are done with their classwork, explore the American holiday of Thanksgiving. It is a major holiday with a day or two off from business and from school. Thanksgiving begins the Christmas holiday season and the day after Thanksgiving is often known as Black Friday. Stores start to sell Christmas goods and hope that their sales will keep the profits "in the black" for the year. If not it may be a "black Friday" for them. Here is a story to share with your students about Thanksgiving,

The Story of the Five Kernels

It was very cold for the Pilgrims their first winter in America. They did not bring enough food with them so food was in short supply. Some days, they had only five kernels of corn per person. Some starved to death, all were starving. When spring came, the Pilgrims planted their remaining corn. The Indians taught them to hunt for meat and showed them which wild foods growing in this strange land were safe to eat. The much needed corn was harvested in the fall. To remember the sacrifice of these Pilgrims, some families place five kernels of corn beside each plate to remind them of their blessings:

1. The autumn beauty
2. Their love for each other
3. Their family's love
4. Their friends, especially the Indians
5. Their freedom to worship God as they pleased

Learning Activity

Below is Bingo to develop vocabulary. Choose from the assortment the activities that will best suit your class. The Thanksgiving Quiz is to follow the reading assignment and could be used as a pop quiz the next week or given to take home and complete after reading about Thanksgiving.

Answers to Fix It

in 1621 the pilgrim governor william bradford proclained an day of thanksgiving
to be shared buy all the colonists and the neighboring native americans

In 1621 the Pilgrim governor, William Bradford, proclaimed a day of thanksgiving to be shared by
all the colonists and the neighboring Native Americans.

In 1621, the Pilgrim governor etc.

In 1621 the pilgrim governor William Bradford

9-11 errors depending how the student chooses to fix it.

THANKSGIVING

stuffing	pumpkin pie	wishbone
friends	thankful	turkey
football	gratitude	Indians
feast	gobble	harvest
family	giving	gravy
fall	nuts	salad
dressing	pumpkin	treasure
cranberries	prayer	traditions
corn	potatoes	Thanksgiving
carve	Plymouth Rock	thank you
blessing	pilgrims	share
autumn	Mayflower	reunion

↔   ↕   \   /   X   +   L   U   C   K   Y   T   □   ■

HOW MANY WORDS CAN YOU MAKE FROM THE WORD
"THANKSGIVING"?

1	18
2	19
3	20
4	21
5	22
6	23
7	24
8	25
9	26
10	27
11	28
12	29
13	30
14	31
15	32
16	33
17	34

Articles **a** and **an**

	a/an		
1		turkey, a big bird we eat at Thanksgiving	
2		apple is a fruit we put in salads and pies	
3		nut	
4		pumpkin we make into pie	
5		family	
6		wishbone big collar bone in a turkey used to make a wish.	
7		Indian, Native American	
8		potato	
9		Pilgrim	
10		apple pie	

THANKSGIVING QUIZ

1. In what country did the Thanksgiving holiday originate?
   a America
   b. England
   c. Scotland
   d. Mexico

2. In 1621, Pilgrims at Plymouth Colony shared a harvest feast with which Native American Indian tribe?
   a. Chickasaw
   b. Shoshoni
   c. Susquehannock
   d. Wampanoag

3. What percentage of Americans eats turkey on Thanksgiving?
   a. 39 percent
   b. 50 percent
   c. 88 percent
   d. 99 percent

4. Where did turkeys originate?
   a. Africa
   b. Central Asia
   c. North and Central America
   d. Australia

5. Where is the annual Macy's Thanksgiving Day Parade held?
   a. New York City
   b. Macy, Indiana
   c. Macy, Nebraska
   d. Pasadena, California

6. Which president proclaimed Thanksgiving Day an official national holiday?
   a. Thomas Jefferson
   b. Abraham Lincoln
   c. Ulysses S. Grant
   d. John F. Kennedy

7. Each year, the president receives a gift of a live turkey and then "pardons" the bird during a ceremony at the White House. What happens to the pardoned turkey?
   a. It is set free to live in the wild
   b. It is served at the president's Thanksgiving dinner
   c. It lives the rest of its life on a farm
   d. It is auctioned to the highest bidder

8. For many Americans, football is as much a part of Thanksgiving as are turkey and pumpkin pie. In what year was the first NFL game played on Thanksgiving?
   Day since what year?
   a. 1920
   b. 1930
   c. 1940
   d. 1950

9. The day after Thanksgiving typically is the busiest shopping day of the year. What is that day often called?
   a. Thanksgiving Friday
   b. Black Friday
   c. Casual Friday
   d. Super Tuesday

10. Which dessert was not part of the first Thanksgiving celebration?
    a. Pumpkin pie
    b. Apple cake
    c. Pecan pie
    e. All of the above

ANSWERS

How many words can be made from the words <u>Thanksgiving</u>?

a	his	signing	vain
aging	hit	sin	van
an	hits	sing	vans
angst	in	singing	vast
ant	ink	sink	vat
anti	inking	sinking	vats
ants	inks	sit	
as	inn	skating	
ash	inns	ski	
ask	ins	skiing	
at	is	skin	
gag	it	stag	
gags	its	staging	
gain	knight	staking	
gaining	knighting	stank	
gains	knights	staving	
gait	kin	sting	
gaits	king	stinging	
gas	kings	stink	
gash	kit	stinking	
gig	kits	skit	
gigs	kiting	skiving	
gin	knit	tag	
gink	knits	tags	
ginks	nag	taking	
gins	nags	tan	
gist	net	tang	
giving	nets	tans	
gnat	nigh	tank	
gnats	night	tanks	
ha	nights	task	
hag	nit	than	
hags	nits	thank	
hah	sang	thanking	
hang	sank	thanks	
hanging	sat	thin	
hangings	shag	thing	
hangs	shaking	things	
has	shank	think	
hat	shanks	thinking	
hating	shaving	thinks	
hats	shin	thins	
having	sigh	this	
hiking	sighing	tin	
hint	sight	ting	
hinting	sighting	tings	
hints	sign	tins	

THANKSGIVING QUIZ ANSWERS

1. a. America

2. d. Wampanoag

3. c. 88 percent

4. c. North and Central America

5. a. New York City

6. b. Abraham Lincoln

7. c. It lives the rest of its life on a farm

8. a. 1920

9. b. Black Friday

10. d. All of the above

WORDS FOR THE BINGO GAME

Autumn or fall - the season between summer and winter
Blessing – a prayer said at a meal, also approval or encouragement
Carve - to cut with care and precision
Corn - vegetable grain eaten by animals and humans
Cornucopia– woven curved horn filled with fruits, grains and vegetables, It is also called a horn of plenty and signifies abundance
Country - land of a person's birth, residence or citizenship
Cranberries - a tart red berry traditionally served with turkey
Dressing or stuffing - seasoned meat, vegetable and bread mixture used to stuff turkey or chicken. Both words are used interchangeably
Family - group of related individuals living under one roof,
Feast – A very large meal
Football - American game always played on Thanksgiving and watched by men
Friends - those attached to others by great affection or esteem
Giving - to offer something to another
Gobble - the sound made by a male turkey; also to eat rapidly
Gratitude or thankful - to appreciate what is done for you by another
Gravy - a salty sauce made from the thickened, seasoned juices of cooked meat
Harvest - process of gathering in a crop, the yield from a crop
Health - freedom from physical, mental and emotional disease or pain
Indians - Native American
Mayflower - the small English ship which transported Pilgrims to Plymouth, Massachusetts, in 1620

Nuts - hard-shelled seeds of many kinds including cashews, pecans, etc.

Pilgrims - English colonists who settled in Massachusetts in 1620

Plymouth Rock – the rock where the pilgrims landed in America in 1620

Potatoes - starchy vegetable, often called spuds; can be baked, mashed, etc.

Prayer - an earnest request or wish to God, a talk with God

Pumpkin - a large, round, orange fruit often used to decorate for Thanksgiving

Pumpkin pie - a sweet pumpkin dessert with a crust

Reunion - getting together with friends or family, often after being apart

Salad – raw vegetables and fruit mixed together and served with a dressing

Share - to give a portion of what you have to partake with others

Thank you – words used to express gratitude for what someone has done for us

Thanksgiving Day - legal holiday in the USA, which always occurs on the fourth Thursday of November, and in October in Canada.

Traditions- the handing down of customs and beliefs to the younger generation

Treasures - something valuable

Turkey- a large American bird, traditionally eaten on Thanksgiving

Wishbone - a forked bone in front of the breastbone in a bird. Two children will get a wishbone and make a wish. Each will then hold one side then pull to break it. The person with the longest side is said to get their wish, but it is only a game.

Lesson 14: *A Christmas Carol* and Character Analysis

Purpose

Students will show their comprehension of their reading by taking a "pop" quiz. Students will learn the steps of doing the Logical Level Alignment for a character analysis.

Notes for the Teacher

Pass out copies of the quiz included in the reading material in the last lesson and have the students complete it to check comprehension and also for you to find out if they are reading and comprehending the material. Then if you can download or purchase it, show Dickens' Christmas Carol Stave One.

You may also want to go over the parts of a Logical Level Alignment Program applied to a Character sketch. In an earlier lesson students were introduced the NLP Logical Level Alignment program to create a pro/con essay. In this lesson they will use the same program in a completely different application, a character sketch. Neurolinguistic innovator and developer, Robert Dilts studied the work of Gregory Bateson on logical levels of neurology. Dilts noted that as people move from the bottom level of environment to the top level of purpose increasing more of a person's neurology becomes involved. The environment level is sensory. Our sensory system inputs to our brain what we see, hear, smell, taste and feel at the place where we are at. Then in that environment we move and become involved as we relate to it. Take as a 'for instance' a child in a field on a running track. It is merely child and a track and nothing more. The child can see, possibly hear, feel and even taste and smell the track but nothing more. Movement is at a deeper neurological level than our sensory input for no longer are we just gathering information about our environment, we are now reacting to it. The child moves his legs and hits them on the track. He may notice that sound arises when his feet hit the surface and that the surface is warm or cool, and hard. Still the foot hits are random and shapeless yet from those movements capabilities arise.

Behaviors do not have a plan or a strategy. They occur naturally. Capabilities reach deeper into our neurology. We plan and shape the behavior. The child begins to move his/her legs in such a way that movement across the track occurs. When we are capable of doing things we the gain beliefs and values about those things we do. As the movement occurs the child reaches deeper still into the neurology of his system and believes that he can run in such a way that he is racing around the track.

The child may enjoy running or may be taking a class where running is required. Soon he believes he can run the track, maybe race his friends, and even enter a race. S/he values passing the course or the feeling of friendship with his friends or the possibility of winning.

These capacities, beliefs and values give rise an identity, who we are. The child becomes a runner. S/he takes on that as an identity. This sense of who we are organizes the levels below as who we are relates to what we believe and value, and that to our capabilities which arise from our behaviors that are a reaction to our environment and basic needs. There is an awareness of what Gregory Bateson called, "the pattern that connects" all of the levels together in a larger whole something bigger than ourselves. As we recognize who we are we begin to see outside of ourselves and take on a purpose that is greater than we are. Our runner desires to encourage others to run and to feel the exhilaration of a healthy body gliding around the track effortlessly making many laps and feeling great afterwards.

Take, for another example a college student taking this class. As you present this to your students, have a bit of fun with it and add things that would make it engaging to your students.

	answers	
Environment	**When and where?**	at a college in this classroom today.
Behavior	*What?*	holding a pencil and sitting tall as /she listens in rapt attention to the words flowing from the teacher's mouth as pearls of wisdom.
Capability	*How?*	to write interesting essays that will engage the teacher and make him/her want to stay up all night just reading the works of the students
Beliefs and values	*Why?*	the student believes he will be a wonderfully creative writer and will make a lot of money selling his/her work around the world
		the student values creativity and the ability to astound the audience with words that sparkle and delight the reader.
Identity	Who?	I am a creative writer
Purpose	"For Whom or What"	The student will spend much of his/her wealth providing classes for underprivileged students and provide them with copies of this wonderful text so that they, too, can become wonderful and creative writers.

Learning Activity

- Write the names of the characters that have been introduced in the first stave. They are thus far: Scrooge, the clerk Bob Cratchet, Scrooge's nephew Fred, two portly gentlemen, Jacob Marley's ghost.
- Students will write a sentence about one character in Dickens' Christmas Carol. Do not put who the character is.
- Pass it to a neighbor and see if they can identify who the character is.
- Or do it as two teams in the class and one team reads one while the other team guesses which one it is.

Answers to Fix It

but why cried scrooge s nephew   Why

why did you get married said scrooge

because i fell in love

"But why?" cried Scrooge's nephew. "Why?"

"Why did you get married?" said Scrooge.

"Because I fell in love."

Lesson 15: *A Christmas Carol* and Outlines

Purpose

Students will begin to write a compare and contrast essay by creating an outline of materials they have researched on the internet.

Notes for the Teacher

If possible, show the students Stave 3 of Dickens' *"A Christmas Carol."*

Talk with the students about how things were different when you were much younger to how they are now. Ask them to imagine life without a smart phone or without a computer. Ask what other things might be different. Next have them think even farther back, to the time of Dickens. Have them imagine and share what they think life might have been like. You might divide into two groups and have the students race to see who can write down the most things that have changed since the middle of the 19th Century. The winners may get to leave the classroom first when the bell rings.

Next prepare them to narrow down a topic by talking about some of the topics they came up with and tell how that topic might be too broad or a good choice. Last have them do the activity to prepare for the homework.

Learning Activity

Have each student brainstorm four topics that they might be interested in writing about on their compare and contrast essay.

After they have all written four topics talk to them about narrowing the topic. Have them choose one topic that they are especially interested in and narrow it down to a single area.

Have them exchange topics with their peers and have the peers tell if they think it is narrow enough for a short essay.

Answers to Fix It

```
ding, dong!  a 1/4 past," said scrooge. counting
ding dong    half past  sayed scrooge
ding dong    a 1/4 two it  said scrooge
```

"Ding, dong!"

"A quarter past," said Scrooge, counting.

"Ding dong!"

"Half past!" said Scrooge.

"Ding dong!"

"A quarter to it," said Scrooge.

Lesson 16: *A Christmas Carol* and Compare and Contrast Essays

Purpose

Students will use their outlines as a base to write an essay comparing something from 18th Century England to today in their home country. Students will begin to learn how to narrow down a topic.

Notes for the Teacher

Show stave 3 of Dickens' *A Christmas Carol*.

The student reading assignment has readings on how to narrow a topic. This is often a difficult skill for students so there is an activity to expand their skills.

In the western culture the time from Thanksgiving to Christmas is the time of the Christmas Holiday. Teach your students about the Christmas holiday and do the Christmas activity below.

A Brief Introduction to Christmas and Santa Claus

Christmas

The story of Christmas begins with the birth of a Jewish baby boy in Jerusalem, Israel about 6 B.C. According to Christian traditions and teaching Jesus was fathered by a God and his mother was a mortal. The boy grew up never doing anything wrong and had extreme compassion for others. When he has thirty-three years old many Jews hated him because they felt he should be a leader in the war against the Romans who had conquered them, but instead he choose to be a religious leader preaching peace. The Jews, angry that he was not going to lead them in battle, turned him in to the Romans on a charge that he called himself a God. It was on a festival day and the Romans had a tradition to let a prisoner go free on the Passover Festival. Knowing that Jesus was not guilty of any transgressions of their laws (and calling himself a God was not against Roman Law) they decided to ask the people who to let free, Jesus or a man named Barabbas who had murdered many people. In their anger the Jews called out to let Barabbas go free and kill Jesus. Christians say that Jesus was innocent of ever doing wrong and was killed by the wickedness of others. They believe that he paid for everything anyone on earth did that was wrong and so everyone is saved and will not go to Hell when they die.

His birthday is celebrated as Christmas. Over the years his birthday, which was likely in April, has moved to December when it was a convenient time in the year with no harvests or planting and it blended in with the Winter Solstice when the sun came back to brighten the world.

Soon after the birth of Jesus, scholars from the east came to see him as he was born King of the Jews. They brought gifts befitting a king including gold, frankincense, a powerful perfume, and myrrh, a healing herb medications are made of. Over the last 2,000 years many more traditions have grown including Santa Claus.

Santa

Your first question may be, "Was Santa real?". Indeed he was. In Russia about 400 years after the birth of Jesus a man named Nicholas lived. He was a good and kind man who looked for things to do for others. Near him lived a very poor family with three lovely, sweet daughters. The custom in the land was for the parents of girls to give the man or his family money when he took a girl to wife. This was called a dowry. The family had no money for a dowry and so the girls remained sadly unmarried. Seeing their plight, Nicholas, one night, dropped some coins in one of the girl's socks or shoes depending on who tells the story. It was enough for a dowry and she could get married. The next night he snuck out and did the same and again the third night so all of the girls would be wed. This was not the end of his good deeds and he was known for all the good he did. Children now get shoes or socks filled with trinkets on Christmas in memory of the good of Nicholas who was sainted by the Catholic Church as Saint Nicholas. Eventually the story was told around the world and his name was changed many times and now is often known as Santa Claus.

Many cultures have a famous person like that and are surprised to learn it was a real person. In China there was a young boy named Lei Feng who was also known for the good things he did. He died early, at twenty one, and someone discovered his journal where he had noted some of his good deeds. Like Nicholas who flies through the air with eight reindeer, maybe all of the stories about Lei Feng are not true but they are based on a real person who lived an exemplary life and has become a model of a good citizen for us all to emulate.

Learning Activity

Narrowing a topic

Give the students a broad topic such as families, countries, business, hobbies, sports, clothes, or entertainment. Give the holiday season, topics such as Christmas tree, Santa Claus, Jesus, ornaments, decorating a house, or traditions could be used in appropriate. Challenge the students to come up with as many sub topics as possible. You might give every group in the class the same topic and see which group can come up with more and make it a contest.

Christmas Card

Put everyone's name in a jar. Have each student draw out a name that is not their own. Challenge each student to write a four line poem for Christmas. Then decorate the page with Christmas pictures or, if you can get them, Christmas stickers. Last, give it to that person whose name they drew out.

Answers to Fix It

D. 11, 2012

dear santa

> i has been good this year   i washing dishs everyday and
> four christmas me wants a doll and cloths and socks an
> shoes. and my mom wants a hat and gloves and scarf

yours truly

mary

December 11, 2012

Dear Santa,

   I have been good this year. I wash (or washed) the dishes every day. (this may be a second paragraph) For Christmas I want a doll and clothes, and socks and shoes. My mom wants a hat, gloves and a scarf.

Yours truly,

Mary

There are several was to correct this. There are about 25-30 errors depending on how you fix it.

Lesson 17: *A Christmas Carol* and Peer Editing

Purpose

Students use their peer edit notes for redo their essay draft into a final essay. Students will learn more about the western tradition of Christmas.

Notes for the Teacher

Show and discuss Stave4 of Dickens' *"A Christmas Carol ."* Peer edit the student essays.

Pass out the Bingo game pages and have the students choose twenty-five words and put the words on their board. Tell them to put their choices in different places than their neighbors. As you call out the words to be crossed out, tell the students a bit about each word to build vocabulary. If you have personal experiences with the word, tell the students about it. The game usually takes 30-40 minutes. You might want to get Christmas stickers or small Christmas candy to use for prizes. It would be nice to have a special prize for the person who gets black out. Always make sure you have extra prizes in the event that 3 or 4 get the same Bingo at once or get a black out.

Learning Activity

Bingo. See individual game papers and the vocabulary words below. Call out the words randomly. As you call a word, make sure you check it off so you will know what words you have used already.

Answers to Fix It

2016 december 2016
dear grandma
I is studying hard at the university and we are learning about western customs and about christmas and it is a really fun holiday and children get presents from a man names santa who is an folk legend
character based on an real person named nicholas who secretly gave money two poor in the 4th century
love
seresa roundy

December 12, 2017

Dear Grandma,

I am studying hard at the university. We are learning about western customs and about Christmas. It is a really fun holiday. Children get presents from a man named Santa, who is a folk legend character based on a real person named Nicholas. Nicholas secretly gave money to the poor in the 4th century.

Love,

Seresa Roundy

There are about 26 errors. There is more than one way to fix this assignment

Handouts and Activity Sheets

Christmas Bingo

candy canes	candles	holly	St. Nick
cardinals	ornaments	fireplace	chimney
cards	presents	love	oranges
Jesus	Bible	carols	caroling
red	green	gold	silver
Reindeer	Rudolf	wreath	garland
Santa	poinsettia	decorations	bells
stockings	gingerbread	mistletoe	nutcracker
tree	nativity	cookies	sleigh

■ ↔ ↕ \ / X + L U C K Y □

You may win only one time at BINGO, but you are still in the game for black-out!

Christmas Bingo

tree	nativity	cookies	sleigh
Santa	poinsettia	decorations	bells
cardinals	ornaments	fireplace	chimney
stockings	gingerbread	mistletoe	nutcracker
reindeer	Rudolf	wreath	garland
Jesus	Bible	carols	caroling
cards	presents	love	oranges
red	green	gold	silver
candy cane	candles	holly	St. Nick

■ ↔ ↕ \ / X + L U C K Y □

You may win only one time at BINGO, but you are still in the game for black-out!

Word	Meaning
holly	An evergreen
fireplace	A stone or brick area made to contain fire. Children hang a stocking by the fireplace hoping Santa Claus will fill it with gifts.
love	Christians believe that Jesus gave his life out of love for us so Christmas has become a season of love
carols	A word for Christmas songs.
gold	The wise men gave Jesus gold as a gift so gold has become a Christmas color
wreath	A decorative circle often made of evergreen leaves, the circle represents eternal life or eternity
decorations	Things we use to dress or adorn our homes, trees and businesses to celebrate the Christmas season.
mistletoe	A plant that has a Christmas custom that if a person stands under a sprig of mistletoe the next person is to kiss them. Of course lovers try to get caught under the mistletoe.
cookies	A sweet that is popular at Christmas time. Often Children leave cookies out for Santa to thank him for bringing them something.
St. Nick	Short of Saint Nicholas, a man from 4th century Russia known and honored for his good deeds.
chimney	The part of a fireplace that Santa comes down. It all started when supposedly Nickolas dropped coins down the chimney to help the girls who had no money for a dowry to get married.
oranges	A popular fruit at Christmas. Often given to children in times long ago to help prevent scurvy, a disease caused by the lack of vitamin C.
caroling	Going from house to house singing Christmas Carols. Often afterwards the carolers have a party with hot chocolate or cider to warm them up.
silver	A metal and color associated with Christmas because it is a precious metal.
garland	A garland is a string or length of something such as tree boughs used to decorate.
bells	Bells on churches often ring with gladness during the Christmas season, hence becoming a symbol of Christmas
nutcracker	The composer Pyotr Ilyich Tchaikovsky wrote the famous ballet called the Nutcracker Suite. Girls all over the world wait eagerly to see or even dance in it each Christmas season and the nutcracker has become a symbol of Christmas.
sleigh	In northern countries people often used a sleigh to travel through the snow. Christmas is a time for visiting relatives and friends and they would use a sleigh to go visiting making a sleigh a symbol of Christmas. Of course Santa goes visiting and uses a sleigh also.
tree	Not just any tree, but an evergreen tree is used for Christmas because it is green all winter symbolizing eternal life.
Santa	One of the many names for Saint Nicholas. Santa Claus, St, Nick and more.
cardinals	Pretty red birds that often fly through northern countries migrating through during the Christmas season making them yet another symbol of Christmas
stockings	Saint Nickolas was said to have put coins in the stocking of poor girls to help them have a dowry so they could marry. Now children who celebrate Christmas hang out their stockings in hopes that Santa will visit them also.
reindeer	In the far north sleighs are really pulled by small strong animals called reindeer. Of course the fairytale Santa Claus would choose reindeer to pull his sleigh also.

Jesus	Sometimes called the reason for the season, it is a celebration of his birth and a celebration of new life.
cards	People send each other Christmas Cards each year wishing people a good year and catching people up on their previous year. They are a way that families and friends keep in touch.
red	Bright and beautiful, red has become a Christmas color
candy cane	A candy, usually striped red and white and shaped like a cane, to remind people that Jesus was known as a Sheppard leading people as a flock of sheep. The sweet peppermint candy was often used to keep children quiet during long Christmas church meetings.
nativity	Most Christian families have a nativity.It is a collection of little figurines symbolizing the story of Jesus birth. Sometimes it is called a Crèche.
poinsettia	This flower came from Mexico and blooms during the Christmas season so from Mexico came this red Christmas symbol.
ornaments	Ornaments are decorations of all types used at Christmas time on trees and all over the house.
gingerbread	Often a holiday treat, gingerbread is a flat cookie that is hard and can be cut into houses and gingerbread men and used to decorate the house and tree.
Rudolf	A story of a Reindeer who was bullied because of his unusual nose. One Christmas Santa chooses him to be the lead deer on the sleigh because his nose glows and will light the way so Santa does not get lost. It is totally fictitious.
Bible	The religious book of Christians, it holds the story of Jesus in its pages.
presents	Another word for gifts, things given to others.
green	A Christmas color representing the evergreen tree, hence eternal life.
candles	Christmas is at the darkest time of year in the northern countries and candles were used most of the day to give light, and hence became associated with the Christmas season. Also refers to Jesus as being the light of the world.

Lesson 18: *A Christmas Carol* and Final Review

Purpose

Students will show the concepts they have learned by completing a final assessment.

Notes for the Teacher

If you are showing the video of Dickens' *A Christmas Carol*, show stave 5 before passing out the final test.

There are three copies of the final exam. You can choose one of the three or use all three giving each student a different copy to help prevent cheating. If you have chosen to, have the students count their words at the end of the five minute essay and give extra credit to any who beat their first of the year score.

Before passing out the exam, remind the student of the following items as they fit your class.

* Check to make certain your name is on your test.

* Put your student number on both sides of test.

* Check to make certain you answered all questions. Go back and check.

* Lose points on comprehension if not on both sides.

* There are fifty errors in the fix it.

* The Meta Modal Challenge will have a simple question challenging it and then a creative answer to your question.

Handouts and Activity Sheets

Below you will find three final tests and three answer keys for you to use.

Test A.	
Challenge it	Everyone hated scrooge.
Expand it	Scrooge
Fix it	Faculty club hotel Shanghai china 2016 25 12 dear english student you worked very hard this year in your writing class and you completed essays on writing about yourself and characters sketches includes obituaries and you analyzed poems and wrote too poems two you also done an compare and contrast essay learning how to narrow down a broad topic and use a outline I wish u a wonderful break yours Truly professor roundy pssea you next term
Discuss it 5 minutes only	What did you like best, reading the book or watching the movie of "Dickens' Christmas Carol?" Why?
Show you know	Make a LLA for Scrooge. You do not need complete sentences

Neurological Level Alignment

		Scrooge
Environment	Answers **When and Where**	
Behavior	Answers ***What?***	
Capability	Answers ***How?***	
Beliefs and values	Answers ***Why***	
Identity	Answers **Who** am I ?	
Purpose	Answers "For Whom or what?"	

Test B.	
Challenge it (Modal Operator of Possibility)	It is impossible for Tiny Tim to get better.
Expand it	Tiny Tim
Fix it	123 candy cane lane north pole 2016 25 12 dear english student you worked very hard this year in your writing class and you completed essays on writing about yourself and characters sketches includes obituaries and you

	analyzed poems and wrote too poems two you also done an compare and contrast essay learning how to narrow down a broad topic and use a outline my wish to you is 4 you to have a wonderful vacation yours sincerely msroundy ps have a great holiday
Discuss it 5 minutes only	What is the value of watching "Dickens' Christmas Carol" after you read the story?
Show you know	Make a LLA for Tiny Tim

Neurological Level Alignment

		Tiny Tim
Environment	Answers When and where	
Behavior	Answers *What?*	
Capability	Answers *How?*	
Beliefs and values	Answers *Why*	
Identity	Answers **Who** am I?	
Purpose	Answers "For Whom or what?"	

Test C.	
Challenge it	You must see a ghost in order to make a change in your life.
Expand it	The ghost
Fix it	123 candy Cane Lane north pole 2016 25 12 dear english student you worked very hard this year in your writing class and you completed essays on writing about yourself and characters sketches includes obituaries and you analyzed poems and wrote too poems two you also done an compare and contrast essay learning how to narrow down a broad topic and use a outline my hope 4 you is 2 have an marvelous holiday. happy holiday frosty the snowman ps u next term

Discuss it 5 minutes only	Scrooge made change in his attitudes. When have you made a change and why?
Show you know	Make a LLA for Bob Cratchit, the clerk.

Neurological Level Alignment

		Bob Cratchit
Environment	Answers **When and where**	
Behavior	Answers **What?**	
Capability	Answers **How?**	
Beliefs and values	Answers **Why**	
Identity	Answers **Who** am I ?	
Purpose	Answers **"For Whom** or **what?"**	

A. **Teacher Key**	
Challenge it (Universal Qualifier)	Everyone hated scrooge. **Universal qualifier is the pattern to challenge "everyone."** **Suggested challenge question** **Did everyone hate Scrooge, might there be someone who liked him?** **The second sentence should creatively answer the challenge question.**
Expand it	Scrooge
Fix it	Faculty **C**lub **H**otel **(2)** Shanghai, **C**hina **(2)** **December 25, 2016 (5** **capitalization, word, day, comma, year)** **(Space 1)** Dear **E**nglish student, **(3)** Indent You worked very hard this year in your writing class. (one way to fix) **(3)** and-You completed essays on writing about yourself and characters sketches **(1 or 2)** includi**ng** obituaries.and You analyzed poems and wrote **two** poems, **too. (8)** You also **did a** compare and contrast essay learning how to narrow down a broad **(3)** topic and use **an** outline. I wish **you** a wonderful break. **(3)** **(Space 1)** Yours truly, **(3)** Professor Roundy **(2)** **(Space 1)** **P.S. See** you next term. **(6)**

	(5) Layout of address, date, closing and signature **50 errors**
Discuss it 5 minutes only	What did you like best, reading the book or watching the movie of "Dickens' Christmas Carol?" Why?
Show you know	Make a LLA for Scrooge. You do not need complete sentences

.

Neurological Level Alignment

		Scrooge
Environment	Answers **When and where**	
Behavior	Answers *What?*	
Capability	Answers *How?*	
Beliefs and values	Answers *Why*	
Identity	Answers **Who** am I ?	
Purpose	Answers **"For Whom or what?"**	

B. **Teacher Key**	
Challenge it	It is impossible for Tiny Tim to get better. **Impossible is a modal operator of possibility.** **Challenge questions could be** **Why is it impossible for Tiny Time to get better?** **If Bob Cratchit made more money would it then be possible for Tiny Tim to get better?** **The second sentence should creatively answer the challenge question.**
Expand it	Tiny Tim
Fix it	123 Candy Cane Lane **(3)** North Pole **(2)** December 25, 2016 **(5 capitalization, word, day, comma, year)** **Space (1)** **Dear English Student, (4)** Indent You worked very hard this year in your writing class. (one way to fix) ~~and~~ You completed essays on writing about yourself and characters sketches **(1 or 2)** including obituaries.~~and~~ You analyzed poems and wrote **two** poems, **too. (8)** You also **did a** compare and contrast essay learning how to narrow down a broad **(3)** topic and use **an** outline.**My** wish to you is **for** you to have a wonderful **(4)** vacation. **(1)**

	(space here 1) Yours sincerely, (2) Ms. Roundy (3) (Space 1) **P.S. H**ave a great holiday **(5)** **(5) Layout of address, date, closing and signature** **50 errors**	
Discuss it 5 minutes only	What is the value of watching "Dickens' Christmas Carol" after you read the story?	
Show you know	Make a LLA for Tiny Tim	

Neurological Level Alignment

		Tiny Tim
Environment	Answers **When and where**	
Behavior	Answers **What?**	
Capability	Answers **How?**	
Beliefs and values	Answers **Why**	
Identity	Answers **Who** am I ?	
Purpose	Answers "**For Whom or what?**"	

C. Teacher Key	
Challenge it	You must see a ghost in order to make a change in your life. **Must is a Modal Operator of necessity.** **A challenge question might be "Why must you see a ghost in order to change?** **Do you know people who have changed without seeing a ghost?** **The second sentence should creatively answer the challenge question.**
Expand it	**The ghost**
Fix it	123 **C**andy Cane Lane **(1)** North Pole **(2)** **December 25, 2016 (5 capitalization, word, day, comma, year)** Dear English student, **(3)** Indent You worked very hard this year in your writing class. (one way to fix) **(3)** ~~and~~ You completed essays on writing about yourself and characters sketches **(1 or 2)** inclu**d**ing obituaries.~~and~~ You analyzed poems and wrote **two** poems, **too. (8)** You also **did a** compare and contrast essay learning how to narrow down a broad **(3)** topic and use **an** outline.**M**y hope **for** you is **to** have **a** marvelous holiday. **(7)** Happy holiday, **(2)**

	Frosty the Snowman **(2)** **P.S. See you** next term. **(8)** **(5) Layout of address, date, closing and signature** **50 errors** **There are about 50 errors**
Discuss it 5 minutes only	Scrooge made a change in his attitude. When have you made a change and why?
Show you know	Make a LLA for Bob Cratchit, the clerk.

Neurological Level Alignment

		Bob Cratchit
Environment	Answers **When and where**	
Behavior	Answers *What?*	
Capability	Answers *How?*	
Beliefs and values	Answers *Why*	
Identity	Answers **Who** am I ?	
Purpose	Answers **"For Whom or what?"**	

Section 2

In-class Assignments

Lesson 1: Lesson of Introduction

Class work

Today you will embark on a new adventure. It is up to you to go through the door.

Discuss It

Teachers open the door. You enter by yourself.– A Chinese proverb

Fix It

Ann anteater eight andy alligaters apples
sew angy andy Alligator eight ann Anteaters ants?

Expand It

The boy ran.

Lesson 2: Character Sketch

Class work

Today you will hear the story of the dolphins and the power of positive affirmations.

Discuss It

Children are our most valuable natural resource.

---Herbert Hoover, 31st president of the USA

Fix It

daily daphne trainned the dolphines at seeWorld theme park in austin texas

hint   World is supposed to be capitalized.

There are about 11 errors. The number of errors may vary depending on how the assignment is corrected.

Expand It

the dolphin

78

Lesson 3: Obituaries

Class work

Today's lesson is about Neil Armstrong, the first man to walk on the moon. If you are not able to come to class, look up information about Mr. Armstrong on the internet before you start your assignment.

Discuss It

This is one small step for man, one giant leap for mankind. ---Neil Armstrong

Fix It

neil armstrng the american astronaut who said   one giant leap for mankind when he became the first man to walk on the moon died saturday august 25 2012

There are about 14 errors. The number of errors may vary depending on how the assignment is corrected.

Expand It

Neil walked

Lesson 4: Directions to Places

Class Work

Everyone enjoys a holiday. Choose a holiday you had recently and write about it. Use colorful words to describe where you went and what you did.

Discuss It

Discuss what you did on a recent holiday such as Autumn Festival. Use an example from your own life and write in first person. You may use the first person words *I, me and my*.

Fix It

My professor seen a lot ov sites during the
mid autumn festival held in china when
the harvest moon are hear

Expand It

the skyscraper

Lesson 5: Writing Directions to do a Thing

Class work

As students when we work on essays we want to use a plethora of descriptive words to make our essay interesting. We want to paint a picture with words to enliven the imagination of the reader. Writing directions is very different. The beautiful and poetic words of an essay entangle the reader of directions. Directions need to be concise and easy to read with no extraneous words. This week we will practice this style of writing.

Discuss It

Use what talents you possess, the woods would be very silent if no birds sang there except those that sang the best.~ Henry Van Dyke

Fix It

directions from the post office to the rupert square

1. exit the post office you are on f street
2 turn to your left (south)
3 go two blocks on f street
4 you are now at the rupert square
if you need help, just call me at
208-123-4567

There is more than one way to fix this.

Lesson 6: Descriptive Essay

Class Work

Today we wrap up our practice of writing directions in a concise manner. In this lesson you get to share about your home town or a town or city you have visited. Paint a picture that will make the reader want to visit the place you call home.

Discuss It

Everyone that went away (left their hometown) suffered a broken heart." -- Annie Proulx

Fix It

how to receive a gift

first, accept the gift
second said thank you
third open the gifts
last says thank you again

Expand It

my town (or my city)

Lesson 7: The Friendly Letter

Class Work

Today you will fix titles and discuss the power of the written word through the friendly letter. This is often a favorite lesson because it brings back good memories of someone you love.

Discuss It

The word that is heard perishes, but the letter that is written remains." ---Proverb

Fix It

Fix these titles

a history of the oriental tradesman

the life of joshua d roundy

its a long road to beijing

There are 15 errors.

Expand It

A letter

Lesson 8: Formal Emails

Class Work

It is important in this modern time of technology that students know how to put together a good email. Students know how to text from an early age and shoot each other quick emails and tweets but there is arising a need to know how to put together a more formal email.

Discuss It

Learning is like rowing upstream: not to advance is to drop back. ~~ A Chinese Proverb

Fix It

402 east 16 street
rupert, id 83350
16th october 2013

dear grandma
and last week I gone to the fabric market and century park and
pizza hut and then I visit with my friend suzi from idaho
in a word it was a wonderful and exciting experience

yours
professor roundy

There are a lot of mistakes and there is more than one way to fix it.

Expand It

email

Lesson 9: Western Culture: Halloween

Class Work

This lesson will look at western culture with a popular minor holiday, Halloween.

Discuss It

If you went to a Halloween party and could dress up however you wanted, how would you dress? Use lots of descriptive words. Remember only 5 minutes.

Fix It

Five little pumpkins

5 little pumpkins sitting on a gate

the 1st won said oh my its getting lat

the second one said, "there are witches in the air"

the 3rd won said but we don't care

the 4th one said lets run and runand run

the 5th one said im ready for some fun

oh-hh went the wind and out went the lites

and the 5 little pumpkins roled out of site

There are about 43 errors.

Expand It

Halloween

Challenge It

You must wear a costume on Halloween.

Lesson 10: Poetry

Class Work

A student of Professor Roundy wanted one day to know what the parts of an orange were called. From her question this lesson emerged centering around fruit.

Discuss It

"One that would have the fruit must climb the tree." ~ Thomas Fuller

Write about a time when you had an experience that illustrates this quote or a time when someone you know had an experience that illustrates this quote.

Challenge It

It is necessary to peel your orange from the stem.

Write a question challenging the Model Operator of Necessity

Fix It

Fix It (no Electronics)

pith contains the fiber us
need two keep hour bodys
healthy?   And it provides
the antioxidants hour bodys
need too fight diseases like
cancer

12 errors (mistakes)

Expand It

The orange

Lesson 11: Writing a Pro/Con Essay

Class Work

This week we will look at an issue from both sides. The issue discussed in the classwork is the One Child Policy in China.

Discuss It

"No other success can compensate for failure in the home." David O. McKay

Fix It

in english their are too kinds of articles definate (the)
and indefinate (a and an)   the is used for a specific
item and a or an is used to refer to a item
tri these sample
the family is going on a outing
an family is going on the outing

Circle the sentence that tells a specific family.

Depending on how you choose to fix it, and there is more than one way, there will be between 16 and 24 errors. The writing is set up properly. All errors are mechanical errors.

Expand It

family

Challenge It

Challenge It Meta Model: Model Operators of Possibility

Modal operators of possibility include can't, impossible, won't, couldn't, and wouldn't

It is impossible to have more than one child.

Lesson 12: Copyrights

Class Work

This lesson begins to cover copyright issues. It is important to be honest in all of our work. We will also address virtues and honesty is an important virtue to cultivate in our lives.

Discuss It

"To practice five things under all circumstances constitutes perfect virtue; these five are gravity, generosity of soul, sincerity, earnestness, and kindness." -- Confucius

Choose one of the virtues and write your quick write on that virtue illustrating it with someone you know who exemplifies the virtue.

Fix It

of the goods made for apple, most are made in china? once apple s brand is added to it and it is exported to the united states it's value doubles he sayed by ben blanchard

There are 25 errors.

Expand It

Respect

Challenge It

Presupposition:

X is assumed true so Y is also true.

All Chinese students are bright so there is no cheating going on.

Lesson 13: Thanksgiving and *A Christmas Carol*

Class Work

In both the United States and Canada the autumn season is a season of harvest and thanksgiving. Both countries have a day set aside for Thanksgiving. It is a family celebration.

Discuss It

Write about one thing you are thankful for and why.

Fix It

in 1621 the pilgrim governor william bradford proclained an day of thanksgiving to be shared buy all the colonists and the neighboring native americans

Expand It

thankful

Challenge It

Write a challenge question for the Meta Model pattern Mind Reading or The Crystal ball.

I know you want to go to the USA for a Thanksgiving Dinner!

Lesson 14: *A Christmas Carol* and Character Analysis

Class Work

You will continue your reading of Dickens' *A Christmas Carol* and do a character analysis on a character in the book of your choice from the list given.

Discuss It

"The best portion of a good man's life is his little, nameless, unremembered acts of kindness and of love." -- William Wordsworth

Fix It

but why   cried scrooge s nephew   Why

why did you get married said scrooge

because i fell in love

20 errors

Expand It

A person I know with good character is_____ because _____

One sentence only

Challenge It

Challenge the Meta model pattern,"I don't know."

I don't know how to think about Scrooge.

Lesson 15: *A Christmas Carol* and Outlines

Class Work

Your final project will be a compare and contrast essay. You will begin that essay with this week's lesson learning the skill of making an outline. This will be a small research project.

Discuss It

"I fear the day that technology will surpass our human interaction. The world will have a generation of idiots." ---Albert Einstein

Fix It

ding, dong! a 1/4 past," said scrooge. counting
ding dong   half past sayed scrooge
ding dong   a 1/4 two it said scrooge

30 errors

Tip: watch paragraphs

Expand It

Long ago

Challenge It

Challenge the universal qualifier.

Things were always better in the old days.

Lesson 16: *A Christmas Carol* and Compare and Contrast Essays

Discuss It

"If you chase two rabbits, you won't catch either one." –an old proverb

For the five minute write relate this to multitasking. Use examples from your own life and the lives of people you know.

Fix It

In western countries children often write a letter to Santa Claus telling him about the good things they have done during the year. Of course children do not really believe in Santa Claus coming to their home and know that their parents are really the source of all of the gifts and presents. Still it gives them a moment to reflect on the good they have done and to remember how it felt to do something good. It provides a draw towards doing more good the next year.

D. 11, 2012

dear santa

> i has been good this year   i washing dishs everyday and
> four christmas me wants a doll and cloths and socks an
> shoes. and my mom wants a hat and gloves and scarf

yours truly

mary

There are several was to correct this. There are about 25-30 errors depending on how you fix it.

Expand It

multitasking

Challenge It

Challenge the modal operator of possibility.

Scrooge will not come to our house on Christmas Eve.

Lesson 17: *A Christmas Carol* and Peer Editing

Discuss It

Write a letter to Santa (or someone else) and ask for something you would want for Christmas. You will have only 5 minutes, no extra time. In the USA people tell Santa about good things they did that year so he will want to give them the gift that they desire (want). This also gives children the opportunity to reflect on the year and want to do even better the next year.

This is a practice in friendly letter skills.

Fix It

2016 december 2016
dear grandma
I is studying hard at the university and we are learning about western customs and about christmas and it is a really fun holiday and children get presents from a man names santa who is an folk legend
character based on an real person named nicholas who secretly gave money two poor in the 4th century
love
seresa roundy

There are about 26 errors. There is more than one way to fix this assignment

Expand It

Christmas

Challenge It

It can't be Christmas.

Lesson 18: *A Christmas Carol* and Final Review

Discuss It

There will be a topic to discuss on your exam. You will have five minutes. Take a few seconds to organize your thoughts first then put them on paper.

Fix It

There will be a Fix It that will be similar to others you have had in your classwork. Review the areas you had difficulty on to prepare for this section of the exam.

Expand It

You will have a word to expand into a well-formed sentence. Remember to use adjectives and adverbs to give your sentence clarity and color. This is a sentence you make up yourself so it does not have to be true and you can be creative.

Challenge It

You will have a Meta Model challenge from the patterns you have learned this term. You will need to question that pattern in a simple sentence and then creatively answer your challenge. We have learned:

- ➢ Model Operators Necessity
- ➢ Model Operators of Possibility
- ➢ Universal Qualifiers
- ➢ Presuppositions
- ➢ Mind Reading or The Crystal ball
- ➢ I don't know

Sources

Blanchard, Ben. (Editing by Ron Popeski). China slams "distorted" View of Copyright Piracy Problem. *Reuters*. Reuters.com. *11* November 2012. Web. November 12, 2012. <http://www.reuters.com/article/2012/11/11/us-china-congress-piracy-idUSBRE8AA04620121111>

Bynner, Witter. Fruit Poem: A Lover. Fruit Poems. *Taste Arts Inc.*2008-2011. Web. 18 August 2014.< http://www.tastearts.com/tag/fruit-poems/>

"Cherish Your Memories." *Elegant Memorials*. Elegant Memorials.com. 2012. Web. 19 September 2012. <http://elegantmemorials.com/funeral-program-templates>

Dickens, Charles. *A Christmas Carol* . *Chapman & Hall*. 1843.

Dilts, Robert and Judith Delozier. Encyclopedia on Systemic NLP and NLP New Coding. NLP University Press.

Frost, Robert. The Road Not Taken. *Poem Hunter.com*. Web. 18 August 2014. <http://poemhunter.com/poem/the-road-not-taken/>

Guest, Edgar E. It Couldn't Be Done. *Poetry Foundation.* Poetry Foundation.org. CR 2014. Web. 23 September 2014. <http://www.poetryfoundation.org/poem/173579>

Lengel, Jim. "Teaching with Technology." *Power to Learn*. © *Copyright 2014 CSC Holdings, LLC. Web. 13 August 2014.*
<http://www.powertolearn.com/articles/teaching_with_technology/article.shtml?ID=22>

McKane,Ruth Christie & Richard. To My Wife.

Oleson, Alexa. Chinese Think Tank Urges End to One-child Policy *Associated Press.* 31 October 2012. Web. 2 November 2012. http://finance.yahoo.com/news/chinese-think-tank-urges-end-one-child-policy-074125915.html?soc_src=copy

Technology Tip Number 170. 180 Technology tips. © 2006- 180TechTips.com. Web. 13 November 2012. <http://www.180techtips.com/170.html>

The Purdue Owl. Purdue U Writing Lab, 2010. Web. 13 August 2014

http://www.memory.loc.gov/ammem/dihtml/diessay6.html
http://en.wikipedia.org/wiki/Dance_in_China

Special Thanks from Debrah Roundy

Bonnie Bird of Idaho, USA for sparking ideas for me. She and her husband spent several years in China with the BYU China Teacher's Program and during that time she developed holiday games to teach her students about western culture. She was my spring board for many of the holiday games you see in the book. Permission to use materials that she contributed to was granted November 19, 2014.